T0419565

Día de los Muertos

Factors and Multiples

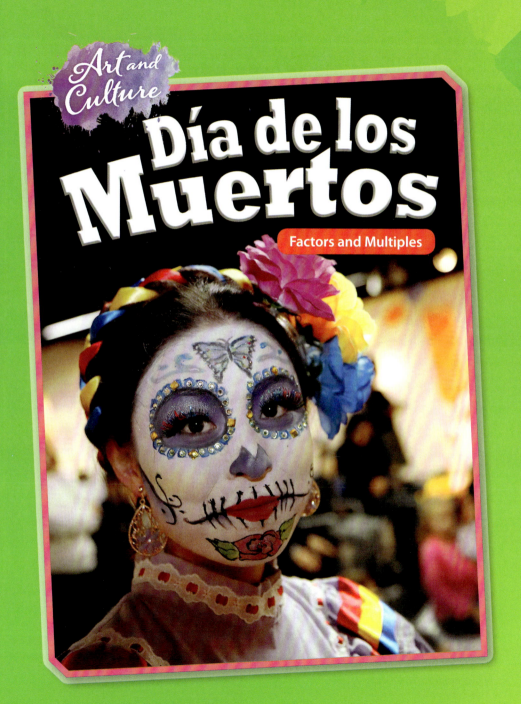

Elise Wallace

Consultants

Michele Ogden, Ed.D
Principal
Irvine Unified School District

Colleen Pollitt, M.A.Ed.
Math Support Teacher
Howard County Public Schools

Jackeline L. Santiago
Teacher
Los Angeles Unified School District

Publishing Credits

Rachelle Cracchiolo, M.S.Ed., *Publisher*
Conni Medina, M.A.Ed., *Managing Editor*
Dona Herweck Rice, *Series Developer*
Emily R. Smith, M.A.Ed., *Series Developer*
Diana Kenney, M.A.Ed., NBCT, *Content Director*
Stacy Monsman, M.A., *Editor*
Kevin Panter, *Graphic Designer*

Image Credits: p.4 Michael Silver Travel/Alamy Stock Photo; p.5 Kobby Dagan/
VWPics/Alamy Stock Photo; p.7 Manuel Vazquez Lopez/Alamy Stock Photo;
p.13 Ethel Wolvovitz/Alamy Stock Photo; p.23 Judy Bellah/Alamy Stock Photo;
pp.24, 24–25 Richard Ellis/Alamy Stock Photo; all other images from iStock and/
or Shutterstock.

Library of Congress Cataloging-in-Publication Data

Names: Wallace, Elise, author.
Title: Art and culture : Dia de los muertos : factors and multiples / Elise
    Wallace.
Other titles: Dia de los muertos
Description: Huntington Beach, CA : Teacher Created Materials, [2018] |
    Audience: Grade 4 to 6. | Includes index.
Identifiers: LCCN 2017011886 (print) | LCCN 2017037566 (ebook) | ISBN
    9781480759336 (eBook) | ISBN 9781425855512 (pbk.)
Subjects: LCSH: Multiplication--Juvenile literature | All Souls'
    Day--Juvenile literature.
Classification: LCC QA115 (ebook) | LCC QA115 .W2585 2018 (print) | DDC
    513.2/13--dc23
LC record available at https://lccn.loc.gov/2017011886

Teacher Created Materials
5301 Oceanus Drive
Huntington Beach, CA 92649-1030
http://www.tcmpub.com

ISBN 978-1-4258-5551-2
© 2018 Teacher Created Materials, Inc.

Table of Contents

Día de los Muertos

This is the story of my family, the Santos! We live in Los Angeles, California. Every November, we honor our **ancestors** who have died. We dress up. We paint our faces. We parade through the streets in remembrance of our loved ones. This is how we pay tribute to Día de los Muertos, or Day of the Dead.

Many people think that the holiday is the **Hispanic** version of Halloween. It's not. Say it with me, "Día de los Muertos is not Halloween!"

Día de los Muertos is a blend of **Aztec** rituals and **Catholic** beliefs. Unlike Halloween, this holiday honors the dead. It is a time of joy and warmth, not fear. We believe that death is not the end. The souls of our loved ones return to us, time and again.

People dress in costumes to celebrate the Day of the Dead in San Antonio, Texas.

ofrenda

Chocolate skulls with colorful icing are used to decorate ofrendas and cemetery tombs.

Preparing the Ofrenda

Día de los Muertos should be called *Days of the Dead*. In many places, festivities can last up to a week. However, most people observe the holiday on just two days: November 1st and 2nd.

This past year has been difficult. My grandma died just a few months ago. She was the life of our family. She was famous for her cooking. She brought us together with her delicious meals. Today, we prepare for her return.

There is still much to do. We are busy cleaning every nook and cranny of our home. The house must be perfect before we set up the **ofrenda**, or altar. Ofrendas are a big part of honoring our dead on Día de los Muertos.

Ofrendas include many items. The way they are arranged can vary. Usually, they include food, water, and flowers. They also include candles and **incense**.

Our ofrenda has two levels. The top level represents heaven. The lower level **symbolizes** Earth. We will decorate our ofrenda with pictures of our loved ones and other items like incense, flowers, and sweet bread. But before we can place anything, I need to find the tablecloth. This will be the base of the ofrenda.

"Rosa, where is the tablecloth?" I call out. "I can't find it anywhere."

"Look harder, Carlos," my sister says. "I'm busy making the **mole** (MOH-lay)."

"OK, OK," I respond. I know my sister wants the mole to be just right. It was our grandma's special dish. She cooked it every holiday. It is a hard meal to recreate, and my sister isn't the best cook!

Food is an important part of Día de los Muertos. Families often bake sweet bread called *pan de muerto*, or bread of the dead.

Mrs. Santo bakes 12 loaves of pan de muerto. She wants to place an equal number of loaves in bags. Find all the possible ways she can prepare the bags by finding the factors of 12. Identify the number of bags and the number of loaves in each bag.

I find the tablecloth and set it on the ofrenda. Now, it is time to place the photographs. I have chosen three photos of my grandma. The first is from her wedding day. She looks so young and happy! The second is a portrait of my grandma with her sisters. The third is a photo of her with me on my birthday. I place each photo on the middle level of the altar.

"Mijo, can you bring in the candles from the garage?" my mother asks. "Oh, and I need you to get the **cempasúchiles** (sem-pah-SOO-cheel-es)." Cempasúchiles are a special kind of marigold. They are not found in our garden. We buy them just for the ofrenda. I will cover the ofrenda with them. Then, a candle will be lit for every family member we have lost.

"Of course. Do you have Grandma's favorite shawl and Grandpa's hat?" I reply.

My mother nods. "Yes. They are in a basket next to the candles."

When we honor our ancestors, we make sure to fill the ofrenda with things they loved. We include their favorite foods, clothes, and other items.

LET'S EXPLORE MATH

Thousands of marigolds are used during Día de los Muertos. They are thought to guide spirits to ofrendas with their color and scent.

Carlos needs to buy 24 marigolds from the flower shop. He wants to know whether he can place an equal number of marigolds on each of the 3 levels of the ofrenda. Is 24 a multiple of 3? Skip-count by 3s starting with 0 to find your answer.

11

Waiting for Midnight

The altar is finally ready, which means that it is almost time to start. All that is left to do is wait. I am so impatient! Outside, there are trick-or-treaters dressed in different costumes. They are eager to fill their buckets with candy. For them, and many others, it is Halloween. For those who celebrate Halloween, the dead are thought to be scary. It is a holiday of thrills and chills. But for my family, the day means something very different.

We believe that at midnight on October 31st, the first souls of the dead come back. These are souls of people who died as children. My family has not suffered this loss. But we do light a candle for those who no longer have family to remember them. November 1st is also known as Day of the Little Angels.

A girl celebrates Halloween by wearing Day of the Dead clothing.

The clock in our hall chimes. It is midnight. We gather around the ofrenda. Rosa lights the candles. The floor is strewn with marigold petals. Day of the Little Angels has begun.

"Mom, I have a question," I begin. "Do people celebrate Day of the Dead everywhere?"

"The holiday is celebrated in many places," my mom smiles. "But it is most popular in Mexico."

"It has a complex history," my dad adds. "The holiday combines Aztec and Catholic beliefs."

I remember learning about the Aztecs in school. They were **indigenous** to Mexico. They built a powerful empire over 600 years ago. Then, the Spanish invaded and brought their **customs** with them.

My parents tell me that the Aztecs believed in a goddess called the Lady of the Dead. They honored the dead for an entire month!

The Aztec world changed in the 16th century. Over time, Aztec **rituals** and Catholic holidays blended. Day of the Dead is a good example of this. We celebrate it on All Souls Day, a Catholic holiday.

Aztec artifact

A man performs in a Día de los Muertos festival.

I want to hear more about the Aztecs, but it is time for bed. Early the next morning we visit and clean my grandma's grave. My father plays guitar while we sing. We stay at the cemetery all evening telling stories about my grandma. My parents tell us stories about what happened before Rosa or I were born. My sister remembers a good story and shares it with the rest of us. She laughs so hard that it is difficult to understand what she is saying.

"Do you remember when she made menudo?" My sister laughs. "She gave it to Carlos without telling him what it was!"

"I thought it was chicken!" I exclaim. "I would never have eaten it if I had known it was cow stomach."

"Your grandma was feisty," my mother smiles.

"I miss her," said Rosa. "I'm glad she will be with us on Día de los Muertos."

A family visits a cemetery on Día de los Muertos.

17

All Souls Day

When I wake the following day, I have a huge grin on my face. It is officially Día de los Muertos! Los Angeles is an exciting place to be for Day of the Dead. There are many people in the city who celebrate the holiday. I can't wait for the parade. People dress up, sing, and dance—so much fun!

Women dance in a Day of the Dead parade in Oaxaca, Mexico.

But first, my family spends time at the ofrenda. Rosa sets a bowl of mole at the altar. She also places the **calaveras** on the ofrenda. These are skulls made out of sugar. Rosa and my mom decorated them with colorful frosting. They are very popular on the Day of the Dead. People use them as decoration and gifts.

LET'S EXPLORE MATH

Rosa and her mother want to place 19 calaveras in equal rows on the ofrenda. Rosa says that there are only 2 ways to arrange them in equal rows because 19 is a prime number. Do you agree? Explain your thinking.

After decorating the ofrenda, my sister sets the table, and it is time to eat. I study her mole suspiciously. But when I take my first bite, I'm surprised. The mole is absolutely delicious! The entire family agrees. Rosa has successfully recreated grandma's famous dish. "Rosa, I didn't want to tell you, but I was worried," my mother laughs. "Grandma's mole is very hard to make. You should be proud."

"Thanks, I guess." My sister rolls her eyes, but I can tell that she is pleased with my mother's compliment.

"I wish we could have mole every day," I sigh, shoveling more of the delicious dish into my mouth.

"But then it would not be special," my father says. "You know this mole is only for formal occasions."

"Tell you what," Rosa replies, "I'll learn how to make something else from Grandma's recipe book for us to try." I grin at Rosa and nod.

mole ingredients

Rosa prepares 15 bowls of mole for a dinner party. She wants to display the bowls on a table in equal rows. Find all the possible ways she can display the bowls by finding the factors of 15. Identify the number of rows and the number of bowls in each row.

catrina doll

These women dress as catrinas to celebrate Day of the Dead.

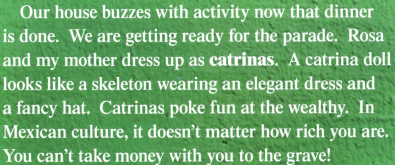

Our house buzzes with activity now that dinner is done. We are getting ready for the parade. Rosa and my mother dress up as **catrinas**. A catrina doll looks like a skeleton wearing an elegant dress and a fancy hat. Catrinas poke fun at the wealthy. In Mexican culture, it doesn't matter how rich you are. You can't take money with you to the grave!

While my family gets dressed, I paint my face. I use black and white at first and add brighter colors later. By the end, I am half skeleton, half kid! Many people will paint their faces today. Some will paint only half their face. The half-painted face symbolizes the strong link between life and death. We only live a short time. Both life and death are celebrated on Día de los Muertos.

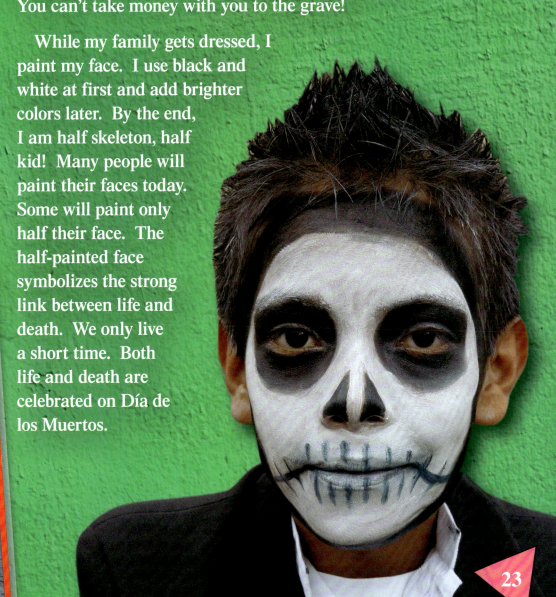

After spending many hours getting ready, our family finally heads to the parade. We wave to other families we know. Everyone has dressed up for the festivities.

There is so much to see! Giant skulls travel through the crowds. Some are so big they take five people to carry them. One group carries a huge **calaca**, or skeleton. Another woman is wearing a gown covered with calaveras. I can't believe how many people there are. Each year, thousands of people celebrate Day of the Dead. It seems as though they are all at the parade!

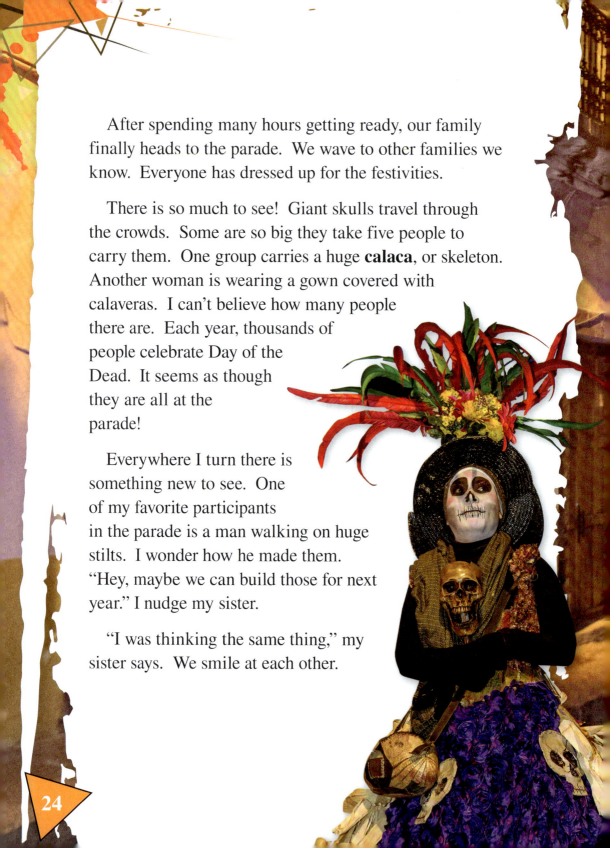

Everywhere I turn there is something new to see. One of my favorite participants in the parade is a man walking on huge stilts. I wonder how he made them. "Hey, maybe we can build those for next year." I nudge my sister.

"I was thinking the same thing," my sister says. We smile at each other.

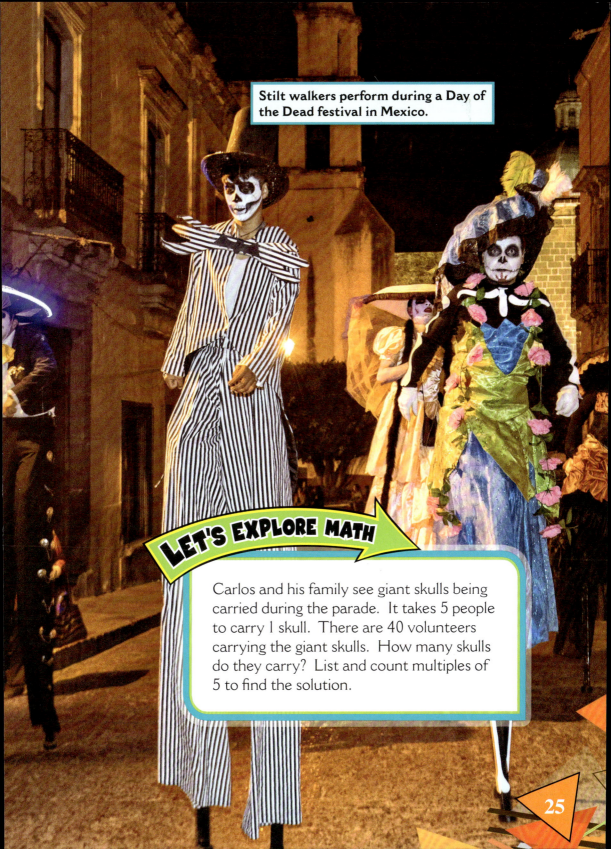

Stilt walkers perform during a Day of the Dead festival in Mexico.

LET'S EXPLORE MATH

Carlos and his family see giant skulls being carried during the parade. It takes 5 people to carry 1 skull. There are 40 volunteers carrying the giant skulls. How many skulls do they carry? List and count multiples of 5 to find the solution.

People burn incense as they parade down a street.

26

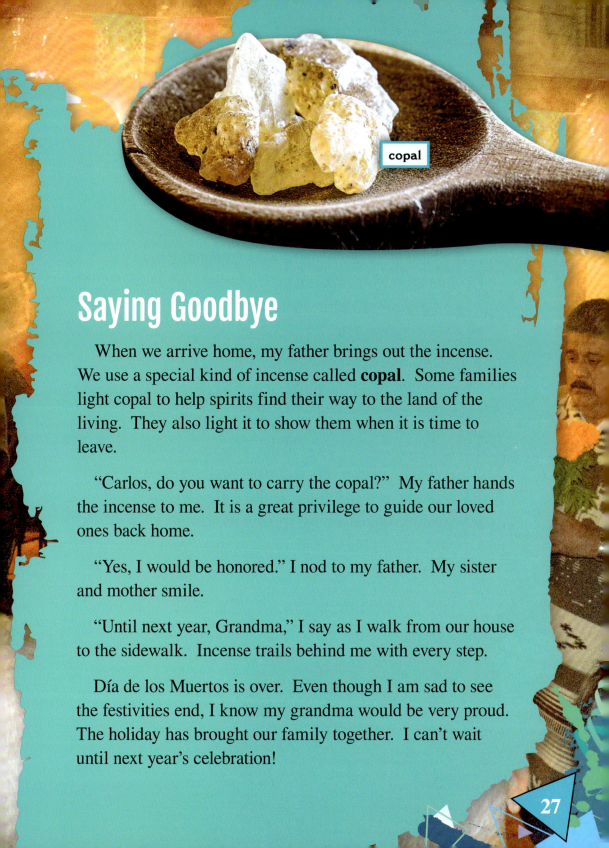

copal

Saying Goodbye

When we arrive home, my father brings out the incense. We use a special kind of incense called **copal**. Some families light copal to help spirits find their way to the land of the living. They also light it to show them when it is time to leave.

"Carlos, do you want to carry the copal?" My father hands the incense to me. It is a great privilege to guide our loved ones back home.

"Yes, I would be honored." I nod to my father. My sister and mother smile.

"Until next year, Grandma," I say as I walk from our house to the sidewalk. Incense trails behind me with every step.

Día de los Muertos is over. Even though I am sad to see the festivities end, I know my grandma would be very proud. The holiday has brought our family together. I can't wait until next year's celebration!

Problem Solving

Suppose you are watching a parade to celebrate Día de los Muertos. Learn more about what you might see as you answer the questions.

1. A group of 16 women dressed as catrinas march in the parade. They want to walk in equal rows. How can the women arrange themselves to make equal rows? Draw a model to show each possible arrangement.

2. A mariachi band also marches in the parade. There are 23 band members. Can the band members walk in equal rows of 4? Explain your thinking.

3. Some people march on giant stilts in the parade. Each person needs 2 stilts. If there are 32 stilts, how many people can use stilts in the parade? Use words, numbers, or pictures to show your thinking.

Glossary

ancestors—family members who lived before us

Aztec—an indigenous people of Mexico

calaca—skeleton

calaveras—skulls made from sugar

Catholic—of or relating to the Roman Catholic Church

catrinas—skeleton costumes that represent rich women who have died

cempasúchiles—a special type of marigold

copal—resin from various tropical trees that can be burned as incense

customs—traditions observed by people in a particular group or place

Hispanic—a person of Latin American descent living in the United States

incense—a substance that, when burned, produces a strong and pleasant smell

indigenous—being born or raised in a particular place

mole—the name for sauces used in Mexican cuisine

ofrenda—an altar assembled during Día de los Muertos that includes a group of objects

rituals—formal ceremonies that are always performed in the same way

symbolizes—to be a symbol of something

Index

Answer Key

Let's Explore Math

page 9:

1 bag of 12 loaves ($1 \times 12 = 12$);
2 bags of 6 loaves ($2 \times 6 = 12$);
3 bags of 4 loaves ($3 \times 4 = 12$);
4 bags of 3 loaves ($4 \times 3 = 12$);
6 bags of 2 loaves ($6 \times 2 = 12$);
12 bags of 1 loaf ($12 \times 1 = 12$)

page 11:

Yes; multiples of 3: 3, 6, 9, 12, 15, 18, 21, 24

page 19:

Yes, Rosa is correct because 19 is a prime number. It has exactly 2 factors, 1 and 19.

page 21:

1 row of 15 bowls ($1 \times 15 = 15$);
3 rows of 5 bowls ($3 \times 5 = 15$);
5 rows of 3 bowls ($5 \times 3 = 15$);
15 rows of 1 bowl ($15 \times 1 = 15$)

page 25:

8 skulls; multiples of 5: 5, 10, 15, 20, 25, 30, 35, 40

Problem Solving

1. Possible arrays:
   1 row of 16 ($1 \times 16 = 16$);
   2 rows of 8 ($2 \times 8 = 16$);
   4 rows of 4 ($4 \times 4 = 16$);
   8 rows of 2 ($8 \times 2 = 16$)
   16 rows of 1 ($16 \times 1 = 16$)

2. No, 23 is not a multiple of 4, or 4 is not a factor of 23. The number 23 is prime because it has exactly 2 factors, 1 and 23.

3. 16 people; Strategies may include skip-counting by 2s, drawing a 2×16 or 16×2 array, or explaining that 32 is 2 groups of 16 or 16 groups of 2.